A STUDEN PARENT'S GUIDE TO COLLEGE SCHOLARSHIPS AND GRANTS

To Robin
Good Luck

RODNEY DUBOSE

outskirtspress
DENVER, COLORADO

A Students and Parent's Guide to College Scholarships and Grants
All Rights Reserved.
Copyright © 2013 Rodney DuBose
v3.0

Outskirts Press, Inc.
http://www.outskirtspress.com

ISBN: 978-1-4327-9765-2

Outskirts Press and the "OP" logo are trademarks belonging to Outskirts Press, Inc.

PRINTED IN THE UNITED STATES OF AMERICA

Acknowledgements

This book is dedicated to my son Jamaal. You put in a lot of hard work to get this far and I thank you for all your sacrifices. Your hard work and dedication has given me the inspiration to write this book.

Table of Contents

Introduction

THIS BOOK IS designed to be easy to read and user-friendly.

A student and parent's guide to college scholarships and grants is for any high school and college student looking for scholarships to pay for their education. The scholarships in this book will explain eligibility requirements and due dates.

In this book you will find a list of private and state scholarships, grants and loans that can be used at any college or university within the United States.

I sincerely hope that after reading this book you will get at least one scholarship or grant to help you pay for your college education. Please email your questions, comments and success stories to: moneycollege4u@gmail.com

Keep your dreams alive and never quit.

Good Luck to all.

How to Use this Guide

FIRST YOU MAY want to search for scholarships that are right for you by looking in the table of contents. Those of you who already know your area of study should start there. For example if you are going to study health care go directly to the section on health care scholarships and start applying for the scholarships. However, you may qualify for additional scholarships by looking in the general or community services section. Most of the scholarships in the book are for programs that require a college degree. Some scholarships require that you come from a particular state; are based on grades; require that you demonstrate financial need; some are designated for particular groups of people such as Men, Women, African Americans, Hispanics and Veterans, etc. Some scholarships just require a completed application.

Since this book was printed some web addresses may have changed. If you use the web address and the link is no longer available please search on the scholarship name.

Here are the top five jobs for people interested in a STEM career:

1. Health specialties teachers, postsecondary

Top skills: communication, science, thought-processing
Annual earnings: $85,270
Percent growth: 15.1 (projected percent increase from 2008 to 2018)
Annual openings: 4,000

2. Computer network architects

Top skills: equipment use/maintenance, science, technology/programming
Annual earnings: $75,660
Percent growth: 53.4
Annual openings: 20,830

3. Civil engineers

Top skills: management, mathematics, science
Annual earnings: $77,560
Percent growth: 24.3
Annual openings: 11,460

4. Medical scientists, except epidemiologists

Top skills: mathematics, science, thought-processing
Annual earnings: $76,700
Percent growth: 40.4
Annual openings: 6,620

5. Environmental engineers

Top skills: mathematics, science, thought-processing
Annual earnings: $78,740
Percent growth: 30.6
Annual openings: 2,790

6 fields that offer the most job security
"150 Best Jobs for a Secure Future," Laurence Shatkin

1. Computer systems design

"Workers in this career field design computer and information systems, develop custom software programs and manage computer facilities. They also may perform various other functions, such as software installation and disaster recovery. They generally work on a contract basis. They may assist an organization with a particular project or program, such as setting up a secure website or establishing a marketplace online, or they may handle ongoing activities, such as management of an onsite data center or help desk."

Software developers, systems software
Annual earnings: $92,130
Percent growth: 57.4
Annual openings: 6,120

2. Educational services

"Education is an important part of life. The amount and type of education that individuals receive are a major influence on both the types of jobs they are able to hold and their earnings. Lifelong learning is important in acquiring new knowledge and upgrading one's skills, particularly in this age of rapid technological and economic changes. The educational services field includes a variety of institutions that offer academic education, career and technical instruction and other education and training to millions of students each year."

Administrative services managers
Annual earnings: $74,970

Percent growth: 19.3
Annual openings: 3,430

3. Government

"The federal government's essential duties include defending the U.S. from foreign aggression, representing U.S. interests abroad, creating and enforcing national laws and regulations and administering domestic programs and agencies. State and local governments provide their constituents with vital services that may not be available otherwise, such as transportation, public safety, health care, education, utilities and courts. Many of these governmental services cannot easily be privatized and are needed no matter how the economy fluctuates."

Social scientists and related workers
Annual earnings: $76,120
Percent growth: 19.3
Annual openings: 860

4. Health Care

"Combining medical technology and the human touch, the health-care field diagnoses, treats and administers care around the clock, responding to the needs of millions of people — from newborns to the terminally ill. Because it meets a lifelong need, and the demand for health care is increasing rapidly, this is one of the most secure career fields."

Physicians and surgeons
Annual earnings: $153,970
Percent growth: 26
Annual openings: 29,480

5. Repair and maintenance

"It's a fact of life that machines and electronic equipment sometimes break down and need to be restored to working order. Routine maintenance services, such as changing the oil in your automobile, often can prevent breakdowns and keep equipment running efficiently. This work provides the livelihood for workers in the repair and maintenance field."

Industrial machinery mechanics
Annual earnings: $40,140
Percent growth: 19.1
Annual openings: 650

6. Utilities

"The utilities field includes companies that generate, transmit and distribute electrical power; distribute natural gas; treat and distribute fresh water; and treat wastewater ... The utilities field is unique in that urban areas with many inhabitants generally have relatively few utility companies. Also unlike most industries, the utilities field imports and exports only a small portion of its product. Because of the essential nature of the product and the relative lack of competition, this field has more security than most."

Electrical and electronics repairers, powerhouse, substation and relay
Annual earnings: $66,270
Percent growth: 10.3
Annual openings: 410

Federal Grants, Loans and Work Study Programs

Federal Student Aid, an office of the U.S. Department of Education, plays a central and essential role in America's postsecondary education community. There are three basic types of federal student aid: grants, loans, and work-study.

Grants do not have to be repaid. Sometimes they are referred to as gift aid. Generally, grants are for undergraduate students, and the grant amount is based on the student's financial need, as determined by the information reported on the FAFSA, cost of attendance, and enrollment status. There are four federal grants:

Federal Pell Grant

Federal Supplemental Educational Opportunity Grant (FSEOG)

Teacher Education Assistance for College and Higher Education (TEACH) Grant

Iraq and Afghanistan Service Grant

Loans are borrowed money that must be repaid with interest. The loan programs allow undergraduate and graduate students to borrow money to cover their education expenses. Parents also may borrow to pay education expenses for dependent undergraduate students. Generally, loan amounts depend on the student's year in school, cost of attendance, and the amount of other aid received. Some loans are based on the student's financial need and others are not. There are five federal loans:

Federal Perkins Loan
Federal Stafford Loan
PLUS Loan for Parents
PLUS Loan for Graduate and Professional Degree Students
Consolidation Loan

Stafford, PLUS, and Consolidation loans are made through the William D. Ford Federal Direct Loan (Direct Loan) Program. Through this program, students and parents borrow directly from the federal government at participating schools.

Work-study lets students earn money while enrolled in school to help pay for education expenses.

Note: Type in the following link to get more detailed information on the available grants, loans and work study programs described above.

http://studentaid.ed.gov/PORTALSWebApp/students/english/funding.jsp

Chapter 1

Technology Scholarships

Microsoft Computer Science Scholarships

A Microsoft scholarship provides a leg up so you can pursue undergraduate studies in computer science and related technical disciplines. You'll join a community of scholarship recipients from the United States, Canada and Mexico who share your passion for technology and academic excellence. It all adds up to achieving your primary goal—making a real difference in the software industry.

http://careers.microsoft.com/careers/en/us/collegehome.aspx

Robert Half Technology Scholarships

Each year, Robert Half Technology and the Association of Information Technology Professionals (AITP) offer two $2,500 scholarships to two outstanding AITP Student Members pursuing studies in Information Technology.

http://www.aitp.org/members/group_content_view.asp?group=83279&id=111037

Federal Cyber Service

Scholarship For Service (SFS) is a unique program designed to increase and strengthen the cadre of federal information assurance professionals that protect the government's critical information infrastructure. This program provides scholarships that fully fund the typical costs that students pay for books, tuition, and room and board while attending an approved institution of higher learning. Scholarship for Service: Full tuition and stipends for undergraduate and graduate students in exchange for service at a federal agency.

https://www.sfs.opm.gov/

Information Assurance Scholarship Program

As a powerful incentive for students to enter the IA field, DoD offers the Information Assurance Scholarship Program. Nearly every day, the United States faces growing threats and attacks against our critical government systems. DoD's mission is to address the Nation's urgent security challenges and to proactively seek solutions to protect and defend our information and information systems. Scholarship funding for undergraduate and graduate students in exchange for serving DoD as a full-time employee after graduation.

http://dodcio.defense.gov/Home/Initiatives/InformationAssuranceScholarshipProgramIASP.aspx

Siegel Service Technology Scholarships

The Siegel / Service Technology Scholarship will be available to students who have demonstrated achievement and a willingness to pursue careers in the service technology fields of automotive, heavy truck, agriculture, aircraft, auto body repair & refinishing, off-highway equipment or related mobility technology.

http://students.sae.org/awdscholar/scholarships/siegel

Intel Science Talent Search

The Intel Science Talent Search® (Intel STS) is the nation's most prestigious science research competition for high school seniors. Since 1942, first in partnership with Westinghouse and beginning in 1998 with Intel, SSP has provided a national stage for the country's best and brightest young scientists to present original research to nationally recognized professional scientists. One of the oldest and largest math and science scholarship programs. Intel STS winners receive scholarships of up to $100,000.

http://www.sciserv.org/sts/

Siemens Competition in Math and Science

Hundreds of thousands of dollars in scholarships awarded annually. From grade school to grad school, Siemens is supporting the next generation of scientists, engineers and business leaders through its educational initiatives.

http://www.siemens-foundation.org/en/resources_for/students.htm

Science, Math, and Research for Transformation (SMART) Scholarship

The Science, Mathematics and Research for Transformation (SMART) Scholarship for Service Program has been established by the Department of Defense (DoD) to support undergraduate and graduate students pursuing degrees in Science, Technology, Engineering and Mathematics (STEM) disciplines. The program aims to increase the number of civilian scientists and engineers working at DoD laboratories. Full tuition and stipends in exchange for summer internships and a year of work after graduation in a DoD lab.

http://smart.asee.org/

National Science Foundation's Robert Noyce Scholarship

$10,000 for undergraduate or graduate students studying to become math or science teachers in exchange for teaching at a "high needs" secondary school for two years after graduation.

http://www.nsf.gov/funding/pgm_summ.jsp?pims_id=5733

NASA Motivating Undergraduates in Science and Technology (MUST)

MUST awards scholarships and internships to undergraduates, pursuing degrees in science, technology, engineering and mathematics, or STEM, fields. The MUST Project is open to all students and is particularly focused on engaging students from underserved and underrepresented groups to enter STEM fields. Each year, the MUST Project will support approximately 100 undergraduate students with a one-year competitive scholarship of up to one-half of tuition, not to exceed $10,000.

http://www.pathwaystoscience.org/programhub. asp?sort=NAS-MUST

AFCEA Educational Foundation

Scholarships of varying amounts will be awarded to students studying STEM (Science, Technology, Engineering, and Math) majors or related fields. Qualifying STEM Majors include: electrical, computer, chemical, systems, or aerospace engineering; computer science; computer information systems; technology management; management information systems; physics; mathematics; bioinformatics; or other majors related to the mission of AFCEA.

http://www.afcea.org/education/scholarships/undergraduate/
STEMMajorScholarshipUndergrad.asp

Chapter 2
Minority Scholarships

Michigan Council of Women in Technology Scholarship

The scholarship program covers one high school senior, one undergraduate-level and one graduate-level college/university scholarship for women who are currently or will be enrolled in college/university-level courses. Also one graduate or undergraduate level research grant, which can be applied to research materials, lab requirements, travel and presentation needs.

http://www.mcwt.org/University_Programs_195.html

Anita Borg Scholarship

For female undergraduate and graduate students.

http://gracehopper.org

Google Hispanic College Fund Scholarship

The Google Scholarship Program offers funds to students studying computer science or computer engineering who are juniors or seniors in college, or pursuing a Master's or PhD. For Hispanic undergraduate or graduate students.

http://scholarships.hispanicfund.org/applications/subsectionID.1,pageID.123/default.asp

Google United Negro College Fund Scholarship

Google is committed to helping the innovators of the future make the most of their talents by providing scholarships and retreats for students pursuing a computer science or computer engineering degree, or a degree in a closely related field with a high volume of computer science related courses. For African-American undergraduate or graduate students.

http://www.uncf.org/sections/ForStudents/SS_Scholarships/scholarships.asp

Society of Women Engineers

SWE Scholarships support women pursuing ABET-accredited baccalaureate or graduate programs in preparation for careers in engineering, engineering technology and computer science in the United States and Mexico. In 2011, SWE disbursed 188 new and renewed scholarships valued at $540,000. Applicants complete one application and are considered for all scholarships for which they are eligible.

http://societyofwomenengineers.swe.org/index.php/scholarships#activePanels_

The Xerox Technical Minority Scholarship Program

Offers a Technical Minority Scholarship between $1,000 and $10,000 to qualified minorities enrolled in a technical degree program at the bachelor level or above.

http://www.xeroxstudentcareers.com/why-xerox/scholarship.aspx

United Negro College

The UNCF Program Services Department manages various scholarship programs. Each program has its own eligibility criteria, open/close dates and required documentation. To apply for a UNCF scholarship, you must apply through the on-line application process. As many of the UNCF scholarships require that the scholarship recipient apply for Federal Student Aid, it is recommended that applicants complete the Free Application for Federal Student Aid (FAFSA).

http://www.uncf.org/sections/ForStudents/SS_Scholarships/scholarships.asp

AWIS Educational Awards

For female sophomores and juniors in college who are pursuing a bachelor's degree in any of the STEM fields.

http://www.awis.affiniscape.com/displaycommon.cfm?an=1&subarticlenbr=340

NASA Motivating Undergraduates in Science and Technology (MUST)

The Motivating Undergraduates in Science and Technology Project, or MUST, funded by the NASA, is a joint partnership between the Hispanic College Fund, the United Negro College Fund Special Programs and the Society for Hispanic Professional Engineers.MUST awards scholarships and internships to undergraduates pursuing degrees in science, technology, engineering and mathematics, or STEM, fields.

http://www.pathwaystoscience.org/programhub.asp?sort=NAS-MUST

DHS Scholarship Program

The DHS Scholarship and Fellowship Program is intended for students interested in pursuing the basic science and technology innovations that can be applied to the DHS mission.

http://www.pathwaystoscience.org/programhub. asp?sort=FEL-DeptHS-Fellowship

Jack & Jill of America Foundation

The Jack and Jill of America Foundation is committed to the ongoing positive development of African American youth and the development of future leaders.

http://www.jackandjillfoundation.org/

AFCEA Educational Foundation

Scholarships of $5,000 will be awarded to full-time students pursuing an undergraduate degree. Students must be currently enrolled and attending either a two-year or four-year accredited HBCU institution in the United States. Students also may be enrolled in an accredited distance-learning or online degree program affiliated with one of these institutions.

http://www.afcea.org/education/scholarships/undergraduate/ HBCUScholarship.asp

Ron Brown Scholar Program

The Ron Brown Scholar Program seeks to identify African-American high school seniors who will make significant contributions to society. Applicants must excel academically, exhibit exceptional leadership potential, participate in community service activities and demonstrate financial need. The applicant must be a US citizen or hold a permanent resident visa card.

http://www.ronbrown.org/Home.aspx

Chapter 3
Engineering Scholarships

American Institute of Chemical Engineers

Each year, students are awarded scholarships based on outstanding academic achievement and their involvement in AIChE programs and activities. Scholarships sponsored by AIChE chapters as well as Fortune 500 companies.

http://www.aiche.org/Students/Scholarships/index.aspx

American Nuclear Society

More than 20 scholarships named after pioneers and leaders in NS&T and other general scholarships are awarded each year to students with outstanding academic credentials. Special scholarships are available to students who have significant economic needs in order to pursue degrees in NS&T. In addition to the scholarships for students entering their sophomore year and higher in college, ANS also provides scholarships to incoming freshmen.

http://www.new.ans.org/honors/scholarships/

American Society for Mechanical Engineers

ASME Scholarship & Loans seeks to establish Educational Funds for the purpose of assisting worthy students in the study of Mechanical Engineering and associated graduate work.

http://www.asme.org/about-asme/scholarship-and-loans

American Society of Naval Engineers

The American Society of Naval Engineers began its scholarship program in 1979 in order to promote the profession of naval engineering and to encourage college students to enter the field. Since the inception of the Scholarship Program, ASNE has since awarded 421 scholarships to undergraduate and graduate students interested in pursuing an education and career in naval engineering. A combination of undergraduate scholarships ($3,000 per year) and graduate scholarships ($4,000 per year) are awarded each academic year.

https://www.navalengineers.org/awards/scholarships/Pages/ASNELandingPage.aspx

National Society of Professional Engineers

Scholarships intended to support talented students studying engineering; these scholarships are made possible through generous contributions from NSPE members, corporations, and friends.

http://www.nspe.org/Students/Resources/index.html

SAE Engineering

Through generous contributions from various individuals, corporations and universities, SAE International awards scholarship money to both undergraduate and graduate engineering students.

http://students.sae.org/awdscholar/scholarships/

Chapter 4
HealthCare Scholarships

Intramural and Extramural Loan Repayment Programs

You do the research. NIH will repay your student loans. That is the idea behind the National Institutes of Health Loan Repayment Programs (LRPs).

http://www.pathwaystoscience.org/programhub.asp?sort=OPP-NIH-LoanRepay

National Health Service Corp Scholarship Program

These student scholarships are funded by the U.S. Department of Health and are geared toward health care students in training. The NHSC Scholarship Program (SP) awards scholarships each year to students pursuing careers in primary care. In return, students commit to serving for two to four years, upon graduation and completion of training.

http://nhsc.hrsa.gov/scholarships/index.html

U.S. Army Health Professionals Scholarship Program

The military is aware of how vital health care services are, which is why they offer military scholarship programs for several healthcare and psychology fields. When you're pursuing an advanced health care degree, the last thing on your mind should be how you're going to pay for it. The U.S. Army can help with one of the most comprehensive scholarships available in the health care field — The F. Edward Hébert Armed Forces Health Professions Scholarship Program. Qualifying students receive full tuition for any accredited medical, dental, veterinary, psychology or optometry program, plus a generous monthly stipend of more than $2,000.

http://www.goarmy.com/amedd/education/hpsp.html

Tylenol Future Care Scholarship Program

Awarding a total of $250,000 in scholarships to forty future healthcare professionals. To those who have committed to a career of caring.

http://www.tylenol.com/index.jhtml

Willard B. Simmons Sr. Memorial Scholarship

All pharmacy students who are NCPA student members are eligible to apply for one of the NCPA Foundation Scholarships

http://www.ncpafoundation.org/scholarships/simmons.shtml

Partners in Pharmacy Scholarship

All pharmacy students who are student members of NCPA are eligible to apply for the Partners in Pharmacy Scholarship per academic year. The student must be enrolled in an accredited U.S. school or college of pharmacy on a full-time basis during the academic term that the scholarship is awarded.

http://www.ncpafoundation.org/scholarships/pip.shtml

Pharmacy Scholars Program

Pharmacy Scholars Program offers funds to students who are pursuing a degree in Pharmacy who have completed one-year of pharmacy school or are in their second year into their pharmacy education.

http://scholarships.hispanicfund.org/applications/subsectionID.1,pageID.150/default.asp

Health Careers Scholarship

Students preparing for careers in medicine, dentistry, nursing, pharmacy, physical or occupational therapy, and medical technologies are eligible to apply.

http://www.iokds.org/scholarship1.html

Brain Track Nursing Scholarship

To help nursing students currently studying to become a nurse, such as an LPN or RN, or to advance their education as a nurse via associate, bachelor, master, or doctoral degree programs.

http://www.braintrack.com/colleges-by-career/lpns#

Bright Futures Scholarship Program

Bright Futures Scholarship Program supports the field of Early Childhood Education by offering scholarships for future teachers. Bright Horizons believe the profession of

Early Childhood Education deserves more respect and support. The scholarship will be a way to encourage students of great promise to continue pursuing their dreams of caring and teaching young children.

http://www.brighthorizons.com/careers/brightfutures.aspx

Barbara Lotze Scholarships for Future Teachers

Undergraduate students enrolled, or planning to enroll, in physics teacher preparation curricula and high school seniors entering such programs are eligible. Successful applicants receive a stipend of up to $2,000. The scholarship may be granted to an individual for each of four years.

http://www.aapt.org/programs/grants/lotze.cfm

Chapter 5

General Scholarships

National Merit Scholarship Program

Junior year high school students who take the PSAT test and meet the cutoff score (varies by state and from year-to-year) can begin the application process for the National Merit Scholarship Program. Approximately 8,200 Finalists receive one of three kinds of Merit Scholarship awards.

http://www.nationalmerit.org/index.php

Coca-Cola Scholars Foundation

The Coca-Cola Scholars Program is open to graduating seniors in high schools in the United States. The Coca-Cola Scholars Foundation supports over 1,400 college students each year, with annual scholarships of $3.4 million through two nationally recognized programs on behalf of the Coca-Cola System.

https://www.coca-colascholars.org/

QuestBridge

The QuestBridge National College Match helps out-standing low-income high school seniors gain admission and full four-year scholarships to some of the nation's most selective colleges. QuestBridge's partner colleges cover the full cost of College Match scholarships using a combination of their own funds as well as state and federal aid. Some scholarship packages also require a student summer work contribution.

http://www.questbridge.org/

Toyota U.S.A. Foundation

Toyota has long supported a wide variety of scholarship programs, many of which focus on students in diverse and underserved communities. Toyota firmly believes in supporting those in pursuit of higher learning to help all individuals achieve their full potential.

http://www.toyota.com/about/philanthropy/education/scholarships/

Robert C. Byrd Honors Scholarship Program

This program, which is federally funded and state-administered, is designed to recognize exceptionally able high school seniors who show promise of continued excellence in postsecondary education.

http://www2.ed.gov/programs/iduesbyrd/index.html

KFC Colonel's Scholars Program

Looking for high school seniors with entrepreneurial drive, strong perseverance, demonstrated financial need and who want to pursue a college education at an accredited public institution in the state they reside.

http://www.kfcscholars.org/

Ronald McDonald House Charities Scholarsl

RMHC wants students to reach their full potentia. ᴖ help them accomplish this, RMHC's network of U.S. Chapters, along with RMHC Global, offer scholarships to students in financial need who have demonstrated academic achievement, leadership and community involvement. Since 1985, more than $44 million in scholarships have been awarded.

http://rmhc.org/what-we-do/rmhc-u-s-scholarships/

Burger King Scholars Program

The BURGER KING® Scholars Program has awarded more than $15.4 million to high school seniors and employees across the U.S., Canada and Puerto Rico since the program's inception in 2000. In 2012 Burger King awarded more than $1.4 million in scholarships to 1,258 students, and introduced and awarded four new major scholarships, including one King $25,000 award and three James W. McLamore WHOPPER™ Scholarship $50,000 awards.

http://www.haveityourwayfoundation.org/burger_king_scholars_program.html

Best Buy Scholarship Program

The program will award scholarships to students in grades 9-12 living in the U.S. or Puerto Rico who plan to enter a full-time undergraduate course of study upon high school graduation. Scholarship recipients are selected based on academic achievement, volunteerism efforts and/or work experience. Up to 1,200 students will each receive a $1,000 scholarship.

https://www.at15.com/contests_scholarships/at15_scholarship/

The Lowe's Scholarship

Lowe's will award scholarships to high school seniors who intend to enroll full-time in an undergraduate course of study in the U.S.

https://careers.lowes.com/college_recruiting_scholarship.aspx

The Central Intelligence Agency (CIA)

If you are a high school senior planning to enroll in a 4- or 5-year college program, or you are a college freshman or sophomore enrolled in a 4- or 5-year college program. Up to $18,000 per calendar year for tuition, mandatory fees, books, and supplies.

https://www.cia.gov/careers/student-opportunities/index.html

Association for Women In Science

Various types of scholarships available

http://www.awis.affiniscape.com/displaycommon.cfm?an=1&subarticlenbr=66

Gen and Kelly Tanabe Scholarship

The Gen and Kelly Tanabe Scholarship is a merit-based program that helps students fulfill their dreams of a higher education. The scholarship is named for Gen and Kelly Tanabe, best-selling authors on education, whose generous donations fund this program. The scholarship provides deserving students of all ages with scholarships that can be used to pay for college or graduate school.

http://www.gkscholarship.com/index.html

U.S. Bank Scholarship Program

The USBSP scholarship is for high school senior ˌ ˌ current college freshmen, sophomore or junior at an eligible four-year college or university participating in the U.S. Bank Student Loan Program.

http://www.usbank.com/student-lending/scholarship.html

Dell Scholars Program

The Dell Scholars Program works with college readiness programs who prepare students with demonstrated financial need for college.

http://www.dellscholars.org/crp.aspx

CVS Caremark Corporate Scholarships

CVS Caremark has a long tradition of supporting the academic aspirations of young scholars.

http://info.cvscaremark.com/community/ways-we-give/employees

Buick Achievers Scholarship Program

Be high school seniors or graduates or be a current under-graduate student. Plan to enroll in full-time undergraduate study at an accredited U.S. four-year college or university for the entire 2012-13 academic year (excluding proprietary and online schools).

http://www.buickachievers.com/

Siemens Merit Scholarship

Each Siemens Merit Scholarship stipend is $4,000 ($1,000 per year). This stipend is distributed each year for up to four years of college undergraduate study.

http://www.siemens-foundation.org/en/merit_scholarship.htm

Discover Card Tribute Award

The Discover Card Tribute Award awards up to $1 million in scholarships annually to high school juniors nationwide. Discover awards up to 300 state scholarships of $2,500 and up to ten national $25,000 scholarships. The scholarships may be used for postsecondary education at two and four-year colleges and trade/technical schools. Winners are selected on the basis of community service, special talents, leadership, and overcoming an obstacle. Candidates must have a GPA of 2.75 or better in the 9th and 10th grade.

http://www.discoverfinancial.com/community/index.shtml#scholarship

Disabled American Veterans Youth Volunteer Scholarship Awards

Disabled American Veterans offers several scholarships for volunteers age 21 and under who volunteer at VA Medical Centers. The scholarships include awards of up to $15,000. For more information, write to Disabled American Veterans, National Service and Legislative Headquarters, Voluntary Services Department, 807 Maine Avenue, SW, Washington, DC 20024.

http://www.dav.org/volunteers/Scholarship.aspx

Chapter 6

Community Servic Scholarships

Prudential Spirit of Community Award

If you've made a difference by volunteering in your community over the past year, you could win $1,000. These prestigious awards, sponsored by Prudential Financial and the National Association of Secondary School Principals, have honored tens of thousands of middle level and high school students over the past 16 years solely for their volunteer work.

http://spirit.prudential.com/view/page/soc/14782?lp=14845

Kohl's Cares Scholarship Program

Every year, Kohl's recognizes and rewards young volunteers (ages 6-18) across the country for their amazing contributions to their communities.

http://www.kohlscorporation.com/communityrelations/scholarship/program-information.asp

Comcast Foundation

Comcast Foundation asks High School Principals and Guidance Counselors to collaborate in identifying the best and the brightest high school seniors in their communities.

http://www.comcast.com/Corporate/About/InTheCommunity/
Partners/LeadersAndAchievers.html?SCRedirect=true

Good Tidings Foundation

Good Tidings supports education by providing education grants to high school seniors in need who have dedicated themselves to extraordinary community service projects.

http://www.goodtidings.org/index.php?id=20

Gloria Barron Prize

The Gloria Barron Prize for Young Heroes honors outstanding young leaders who have made a significant positive difference to people and our planet.

http://www.barronprize.org/

Disneyland Resort Scholarship Program

The Disneyland Resort Scholarship Program provides scholarships to students with great potential, financial need, strong academic demonstration and community/civic involvement.

http://publicaffairs.disneyland.com/education/youth-scholarships/

DoSomething.org Scholarships

Scholarships recognize everyday teens that are taking action and making a difference in their community.

http://www.dosomething.org/scholarships

The Nordstrom Scholarship

Plan on attending an accredited four-year col
versity during the four years over which the scholarship ~~
distributed. The scholarship is paid out in equal installments
of $2,500.

http://shop.nordstrom.com/c/nordstrom-cares-scholarship?cm_
ven=google&cm_cat=scholarship&cm_pla=scholarship2012&cm_
ite=scholarships

Chapter 7
Scholarships for Disabilities or Illness

National Collegiate Cancer Foundation Scholarship

The National Collegiate Cancer Foundation was established to provide services and support to young adults whose lives have been impacted by cancer and who have continued with their education throughout treatment or after their treatment.

http://www.collegiatecancer.org/scholarships.html

Patient Advocate Foundation

The purpose of our scholarships is to provide support to individuals, under the age of 25, who have been diagnosed with or treated for cancer and/or a chronic/life threatening disease within the past 5 years.

http://www.patientadvocate.org/index.php?p=69

Anne Ford and Allegra Ford Scholarships

The Anne Ford and Allegra Ford Scholarships offer financial assistance to graduating seniors with documented learning disabilities (LD) who are pursuing post-secondary education.

http://www.ncld.org/about-us/scholarships-aamp-awards/
the-anne-ford-and-allegra-ford-scholarship-award

Marion Huber Learning Through Listening

Awards are available to high school seniors with LD who demonstrate leadership skills, scholarship, and a high level of service to others; must be a member of Recording for the Blind and Dyslexic (RFB&D).

http://www.learningally.org/

William L. Ritchie Learning Through Listening Award

Presented to a Learning Ally member in the DC Metropolitan area with learning disabilities or visual impairments who, through persistence and determination, has overcome obstacles to accomplish his or her goals.

http://www.learningally.org/

RISE Scholarship Foundation

The Rise Scholarship Foundation, Inc. was established in 2010 to reward students with learning disabilities, who have shown determination, self-advocacy and success in overcoming their difficulties and are pursuing post-secondary education. Rise Scholarship Foundation Inc. aims to offer meaningful scholarships to award the success of students, to bring awareness, and education to the subject of learning disabilities.

http://risescholarshipfoundation.org/

National Federation of the Blind Educator of Tomorrow Award

Open to legally blind students planning a career in elementary, secondary, or postsecondary teaching.

http://nfb.org/scholarship-list

Chapter 8
Scholarship for Military Children

Scholarships for Military Children Program

The Scholarships for Military Children Program was created in recognition of the contributions of military families to the readiness of the fighting force and to celebrate the role of the commissary in the military family community.

http://www.militaryscholar.org/sfmc/index.html

The American Patriot Freedom Scholarship Program

Established in 2006 as a way to say "thank you" to our troops, and to offer educational assistance for their dependent children.

http://www.homefrontamerica.org/oohrahhome.htm

DRS Guardian Scholarship Fund

The DRS Guardian Scholarship Fund provides college scholarships to the children of National Guardsmen killed during service to their country since September 11, 2001. The fund provides up to $6,250 per year to selected students attending a four-year institution or a two-year program at a community college or technical school.

http://www.drsguardianfund.org/

Waldorf College

Scholarships will be awarded to the spouse and child of an active military man or woman and to the spouse or child of active public safety personnel.

http://www.waldorf.edu/Online/Tuition---Financing/Scholarships/Hero-Behind-the-Hero

ThanksUSA Scholarship

The ThanksUSA Scholarship is available to dependent children (age of 24 and under) and spouses of active-duty U.S. military service personnel.

http://www.thanksusa.org/main/index.html

Montgomery GI Bill

The Montgomery GI Bill is available to active duty military veterans, Selected Reserve military personnel, and dependents of military veterans who are permanently disabled or deceased due to a service-related condition.

http://www.gibill.va.gov/

Navy Supply Corps Foundation Scholarship

The scholarship program provides financial assistance to family members (child, grandchild or spouse) of a qualifying Navy Supply Corps officer or supply enlisted member.

https://www.usnscf.com/programs/index.aspx

AFCEA Military Personnel/Dependents Scholarships

The Educational Foundation offers several scholarships designated for military personnel. The common military personnel/dependents application allows students to be considered for all of the scholarships.

http://www.afcea.org/education/scholarships/undergraduate/military.asp

Disabled American Veterans Youth Volunteer Scholarship Awards

Disabled American Veterans offers several scholarships for volunteers age 21 and under who volunteer at VA Medical Centers. The scholarships include awards of up to $15,000. For more information, write to Disabled American Veterans, National Service and Legislative Headquarters, Voluntary Services Department, 807 Maine Avenue, SW, Washington, DC 20024.

http://www.dav.org/volunteers/Scholarship.aspx

Chapter 9
Education Scholarships

Common Knowledge Scholarship Foundation

All U.S. high school, college, and graduate students are eligible (parents can compete, too).

http://www.cksf.org/index.cfm?Page=Scholarships

Judith Cary Leadership Memorial Scholarship

JCLMS Is awarded to a student who is working either full time or part time toward special needs certification or an undergraduate or graduate degree in some field of Special Education.

http://www.mosssociety.org/page.php?id=29

AFCEA Educational Foundation

AFCEA International and the AFCEA Educational Foundation are expanding the Science, Technology, Engineering and Math (STEM) Teacher Scholarship Program for the second year in a row to help address the growing shortage of young Americans educated in STEM subjects.

http://www.afcea.org/education/scholarships/undergraduate/TeachersScholarship.asp

Applegate-Jackson-Parks Future Teacher Scholarship

Applicants are limited to graduate or undergraduate students majoring in education in institutions of higher learning throughout the United States.

http://www.nilrr.org/resources/scholarship-application/

American Montessori Society

Every year, the American Montessori Society awards teacher education scholarships to aspiring Montessori teachers.

http://www.amshq.org/

Zeta Phi Beta Sorority

Available to college Freshmen, Sophomores, Juniors, Seniors and graduating high school seniors planning to enter college in the Fall.

http://www.zpbnef1975.org/

BrainTrack scholarships

BrainTrack scholarships provide funding for education to students who are pursuing a career as either an elementary, middle school, or secondary school teacher.

http://www.braintrack.com/colleges-by-career/ elementary-school-teachers#

Chapter 10

Historically Black Colleges and Universities-(HBCU)

HBCUS ARE A source of accomplishment and great pride for the African American community as well as the entire nation. HBCUs offer all students, regardless of race, an opportunity to develop their skills and talents. These institutions train young people who go on to serve domestically and internationally in the professions as entrepreneurs and in the public and private sectors. Please contact the schools below to obtain information regarding the scholarships they offer.

Alabama A&M University
Normal, Alabama
www.aamu.edu

Alabama Agricultural and Mechanical University is one of the land-grant Black Colleges providing baccalaureate and graduate studies to individuals interested in developing scholastic, professional, and technical skills. It is one of two four-year public universities in Alabama on the White House Initiative on Historical Black Colleges and Universities list of HBCUs. It provides excellent education to capable students with previously limited educational access by fully integrating technology into university life.

Alabama State University
Montgomery, Alabama
334-229-4100
www.alasu.edu

Alabama State University is one of two public four-year historically black colleges in Alabama. Nine freed slaves known as the "Marion Nine" created this school almost a century and a half ago. The university offers 31 bachelor's degrees and 11 master's degrees. Well-respected among Historical Black Colleges and Universities, they are known for their Marching Hornets band. Like other HBCU colleges and African American Universities, they offer a unique learning environment.

Albany State University
Albany, Georgia
229-430-4600
www.asurams.edu

Founded in 1903, Albany State University is one of three historical black colleges & universities in Georgia. With over 4,000 students, Albany State University is a 1st tier school among Black Colleges and African American Universities. Emphasizing liberal arts programs, this four-year, public HBCU was started by Joseph Winthrop Holley, inspired by W. E. B. Du Bois. Albany State's primary mission of creating outstanding citizens is reflected in their motto: "Potential. Realized."

Alcorn State University
Lorman, Mississippi
601-877-6100
www.alcorn.edu

Founded in 1871, Alcorn State University ranks 26th, nationwide, among historical black colleges & universities. With over 2,900 students, Alcorn State University offers degrees in liberal arts and sciences and is a top choice among HBCU and African American Universities. Additional campuses located in Natchez and Vicksburg offer MBA and Nursing concentrations. Alcorn State University has quickly become known among black colleges for creating leaders in fields including education, human services and nursing.

Bennett College
Greensboro, North Carolina
336-517-2100
www.bennett.edu

One of only a few private women's colleges in the region, Bennett College serves over 600 female students. Located in Greensboro, North Carolina, Bennett College is a four-year, HBCU liberal arts school offering 24 degree programs. Ranking 16th among other black colleges and African American universities, Bennett College prides itself on the academic achievements its students and faculty have accomplished. Bennett College began by educating newly freed slaves.

Bluefield State College
Bluefield, WV
Telephone: 304-327-4000
www.bluefieldstate.edu

Established in 1895, Bluefield State College is dedicated to providing an excellent learning experience for all students in the area. Like other historical black colleges & universities, it wasn't integrated until the 1950's but has always prided itself on its core values of excellence, community diversity and growth. As an HBCU, Bluefield State College stands out not just amongst African American universities and black colleges, but all venues of higher education.

Bowie State University
Bowie, Maryland
301-860-4000, 1-877-77-BOWIE
http://www.bowiestate.edu

Since its 1865 trailblazing beginning as one of America's few Black colleges, Bowie State University has evolved into a multi-level degree school. As an HBCU, or historical black colleges & universities, it has an ethnically varied faculty and student population. As part of the network of African American universities, it gives students of color in-depth tools for exploring their own culture while preparing them to work in America's diverse society.

Central State University
Wilberforce, Ohio
937-376-6011
http://www.centralstate.edu

One of the oldest HBCU in America, Central State University has a long tradition of extra-curricular and academic excellence. Like many other historical black colleges & universities, CSU began as a center for teacher education. As one of many African American universities in the country, CSU stands out as a leader in the field of urban education. Also, CSU is one of few black colleges offering graduate degree programs.

Cheyney University of Pennsylvania
Cheyney, Pennsylvania
(610)399-2275
www.cheyney.edu

Cheyney University of Pennsylvania is the oldest of the Black Colleges and African American Universities on the list of Historical Black Colleges & Universities (HBCU) in America. It was founded in 1837 by Richard Humphreys. Cheyney offers baccalaureate degrees in over 30 disciplines and a Master's Degree in education. Graduates of Cheyney have assumed leadership roles in the fields of government, education, law, science, and journalism, as well as other areas.

Claflin University
Orangeburg, South Carolina
(803)535-5000
www.claflin.edu

Claflin University, one of many traditionally African American Universities and Black Colleges on the list of Historical Black Colleges & Universities (HBCU), is affiliated with The United Methodist Church and offers undergraduate and graduate degrees. Undergraduate degrees provide a foundation in the liberal arts, while the graduate program allows students to increase their specialization in specific fields of study as they prepare to take roles of leadership in their communities and chosen fields.

Clark Atlanta University
SW Atlanta, Georgia
(800)688-3228
www.cau.edu

Clark Atlanta University is one of many African American Universities on the Historical Black Colleges and Universities (HBCU) list. Atlanta University was one of the original Black Colleges providing teachers and librarians to southern schools. In 1988, Clark College and Atlanta University merged forming Clark Atlanta University. Clark Atlanta University is dedicated to developing students intellectually and personally, preparing them to be leaders in their communities and fields of study.

Concordia College
Year Founded: 1922
Selma, Alabama
(334)-874-5700
www.concordiaselma.edu

Concordia College, Selma, is one of the 10 universities operated by the Missouri Synod of the Lutheran Church. A member of the country's Historical Black Colleges & Universities (HBCU), Concordia College, Selma, while considered as one of the nation's African American universities or black colleges, represents a diverse racial, geographic and economic cross-section of students. It is the only HBCU in the Concordia system.

Coppin State University
Year Founded: 1900
Baltimore, MD
(410) 951-3000 / (800) 635-3674
www.coppin.edu

Coppin State University is one of the Historical Black Colleges & Universities (HBCU). Coppin is one of the African American universities offering courses at the undergraduate and graduate levels. Like many black colleges, Coppin has famous alumni in such fields as law enforcement (Bishop L. Robinson), politics (Vera Welcome), and professional sports (Larry Stewart).

Delaware State University
Year Founded: 1891
Dover, DE
(302) 857-6060 daytime / (302) 857-6290 evening
www.desu.edu

Delaware State University is one of the Historical Black Colleges & Universities (HBCU). DSU is one of the African American universities that offers degrees through the doctoral level. Like many black colleges, DSU has famous alumni in such fields as politics (Wayne Gilchrest), the media (Maxine Lewis), and professional sports (Shaheer McBride).

Dillard University
Year Founded: 1869
New Orleans, LA
(504) 283-8822
www.dillard.edu

Dillard University, one of the Historical Black Colleges & Universities (HBCU), was ranked as one of the top ten HBCUs among African American universities, and as one of the top ten liberal arts schools. Like many black colleges, DU has famous alumni in such fields as medicine (Mitchell Spellman), law (Revius Ortique), and higher education (Dr. Sandra Harris-Hooker).

Edward Waters College
Year Founded: 1866
Jacksonville, FL
(904) 470-8000 / (888) 898-3191
www.ewc.edu

Edward Waters College offers undergraduate degrees. Edward Water College is one of the Historical Black Colleges & Universities (HBCU) and, as is the case with African American universities throughout the country, serves students who may otherwise find higher education inaccessible. Like many black colleges, EWC has a racially and socio-economically diverse student body.

Elizabeth City State University
Year Founded: 1891
Elizabeth City, NC
(252) 335-3400
www.ecsu.edu

Elizabeth City State University, one of the Historical Black Colleges & Universities (HBCU), maintains a student-centered environment and approach to learning. ECSU is one of the accredited African American universities to offer courses in a number of fields. Like many black colleges, ECSU has alumni of notoriety such as Larry Johnson, Sr., and Johnnie Walton, who have gone on to be recruited by professional ball clubs.

Fayetteville State University
Year Founded: 1867
Fayetteville, NC
(910) 672-1111
http://www.uncfsu.edu/

Fayetteville State University, one of the Historical Black Colleges & Universities (HBCU), has become a highly respected postsecondary institution within the University of North Carolina System. Fayetteville State is one of the fully accredited African American universities to offer courses in a number of fields. Like many black colleges, FSU has a number of alumni who have become professional ball players, such as Blenda Gay and Sylvester "Junkyard Dog" Ritter.

Fisk University
Year Founded: 1886
Nashville, TN
(615) 329-8500
www.fisk.edu

Fisk University, one of the historical black colleges & universities (HBCU), has been ranked by Princeton Review among the top 15 percent of the nation's universities. Fisk is one of the fully accredited African American universities to offer courses in several fields at undergraduate and graduate levels. Like many black colleges, Fisk has notable alumni, including W.E.B. DuBois, Ida B. Wells, Percy Julian, John Hope Franklin, Alma Powell and Mandisa.

Florida A&M University
Year Founded: 1887
Tallahassee, FL
(850) 599-3000
www.famu.edu

Florida A&M University is one of the Historical Black Colleges & Universities (HBCU), is one of the State University System of Florida's institutions. FAMU is one of the fully accredited African American universities to offer courses in the undergraduate, graduate, and doctoral levels. Like many black colleges, FAMU has a number of alumni who have achieved positions of notoriety within their respective fields.

Florida Memorial University
Year Founded: 1879
Miami Gardens, FL
(305) 626-3600
www.fmuniv.edu

Florida Memorial University offers courses in a number of fields. As one of the Historical Black Colleges & Universities (HBCU), it has a stellar track record for graduating students who become teachers. Like many black colleges/African American universities, FMU has many alumni who have achieved positions of infamy in their respective fields, such as Barrington Irving, Jr. (the first and youngest black pilot to fly around the globe solo).

Fort Valley State University
Year Founded: 1890
Valley, Georgia
478-825-6211
www.fvsu.edu

For 120 years, Fort Valley State University has built a student body rich in African-American culture. One of three Historical Black Colleges & Universities in Georgia, it offers 50 bachelor and masters degrees. This HBCU boasts the second largest public campus not only among African American universities, but in Georgia also. Like many black colleges, it encourages students to build a strong commitment to personal and intellectual growth.

Grambling State University
Year Founded: 1901
Grambling, Louisiana
1-800-569-4714
www.gram.edu

Grambling State University is a leader among Historical Black Colleges & Universities with a 384-acre campus. The school is one of many African American universities home to legendary football coaches like Eddie Robinson. The HBCU offers 46 academic programs across a variety of subjects, with nationally-recognized excellence nursing, business, computer science and education. It was the first of the black colleges to host a sitting President in its marching band.

Hampton University
Year Founded: 1868
Hampton, Virginia
(757) 727-5000
www.hamptonu.edu

Hampton University is one of oldest privately funded historical black colleges & universities on the east coast. This well-established HBCU offers undergrad, masters and doctoral courses in technical and liberal arts fields. Hampton University has been rated among the top African American universities in the world, with a community of students from 35 countries and territories and nearly every state in America, making it one of the most popular black colleges.

Harris-Stowe University
Year Founded: 1857
St. Louis, Missouri
(314) 340-3366
http://www.hssu.edu

Harris-Stowe University, formerly Harris-Stowe College, is the first of the Historical Black Colleges & Universities to be an education institution for public teachers. With HBCU, they are one of the oldest black colleges, their degree programs focus on education. As many African American universities, they currently offer 12 different academic studies in Information Systems, Computer Technology, Business Administration, Urban Specialization, Teacher Education, and General Education.

Howard University
Year Founded: 1867
Washington, DC
(202) 806-6100
www.howard.edu

Howard University, one of the great African American universities and flagship of the Historical Black Colleges & Universities (HBCU), offers a comprehensive set of academic programs. The distinguished black college has a long list of notable alumni, including poet Toni Morrison, actress Phylicia Rashad, Sen. Ed Brooke, Mayor David Dinkins, Ambassador Patricia Harris and many others. It is located on 258 acres in the vibrant Washington, D.C.

Jackson State University
Year Founded: 1877
Jackson, Mississippi
(800) 848-8817
www.jsums.edu

A member of the 105 Historical Black Colleges & Universities (HBCUs), Jackson State University has grown from one of many small black colleges in the late 1800s to one of the major African American universities today. JCU welcomes capable students of all diverse backgrounds who strive for excellence. JCU has built a reputation for its achievements in computational computing, education and human development, communications technology, homeland security and nanotechnology.

Johnson C. Smith University
Year Founded: 1867
Charlotte, North Carolina
(704) 378-1000
www.jcsu.edu

Johnson C. Smith University (JCSU), a member of the 105 Historical Black Colleges and Universities (HBCUs) in the United States, is one of the Best Comprehensive Colleges in the South. Historically a Black College, JCSU is ranked highly among its fellow HBCUs and other African American Universities and has a great reputation for its technological integration. JCSU currently provides laptop computers to every student.

Kentucky State University
Year Founded: 1886
Frankfort, KY
(502) 597-6000
http://www.kysu.edu

Kentucky State University, Kentucky's smallest public university, has proud history as one of the country's first black colleges. Its 900-acre campus features historic and state-of-the-art buildings, and its location in the state's capital allows KSU, one of the Historical Black Colleges & Universities (HBCU), to offer unique government internships. African American University KSU has progressed to become the most diverse public institution in the state.

Lane College
Year Founded: 1882
Jackson, Tennessee
(731) 426-7500
www.lanecollege.edu

Founded in 1882 and established primarily for the education of freed slaves and black college, Lane College today flourishes as a small, private, coeducational, liberal arts center of higher learning. Along with other distinguished African American universities, Lane College is a member of the Historical Black Colleges & Universities (HBCUs). The Lane College faculty work together with students to provide a culture of technology throughout their educational experience.

Langston University
Year Founded: 1897
Langston, Oklahoma
(877) 466-2231
www.lunet.edu

Founded in 1897 as one of many black colleges and African American universities, Langston University is a part of the nation's Historical Black Colleges & Universities (HBCUs). Langston University has developed an international reputation for excellence in the field of agricultural research. Langston University currently maintains an open door admissions policy, enrolling a diverse student body and strives to educate individuals to become leaders in their communities.

LeMoyne-Owen College
Year Founded: 1871
Memphis, Tennessee
(313) 862-6300
www.lewiscollege.edu

Founded in 1928 and located in Detroit, Michigan, Lewis College of Business is one of many black colleges, distinguished by its inclusion in the Historical Black Colleges & Universities (HBCU). Lewis College of Business offers business and liberal arts degrees. Lewis College of Business seeks to provide socially relevant applications of knowledge, as do other African American universities.

Lincoln University
Year Founded: 1854
Chester County, PA
(800) 790-0191
http://www.lincoln.edu/

Lincoln University, founded in 1854, was the first Historically Black College (HBCU) in the US. In the African American university's 150 year-history, alumni include Thurgood Marshall, Langston Hughes and the Presidents of Nigeria and Ghana. Lincoln offers undergraduate and graduate programs and its 422-acre campus, located in rolling Pennsylvania between Philadelphia and Baltimore, reveals an inviting and vibrant black college.

Livingstone College
Year Founded: 1879
Salisbury, North Carolina
(800) 835-3435
www.livingstone.edu

Founded in 1879 as a black college, Livingstone College is one of the nation's 105 Historical Black Colleges and Universities (HBCUs). Livingstone College is a private, four-year college affiliated with the African Methodist Episcopal Zion Church. Livingstone College offers programs to award the B.A., B.S., and other degrees. Notable alumni of this African American university include Ben Coates and Wilmont Perry, both former NFL players.

Miles College
Year Founded: 1898
Birmingham, AL
(205) 923-2771
www.miles.edu

A member of the United Negro Fund, Miles College was established in Fairfield, Ala. as a black college. Recognized as one of the nation's Historical Black Colleges and Universities (HBCU), Miles College maintains an open admissions policy and offers liberal arts degrees to students as one of the elite African American universities. Notable alumni of Miles College include business leaders, teachers, physicians and legislators.

Mississippi Valley State University
Year Founded: 1950
Itta Bena, Mississippi
(662) 254-3347
www.mvsu.edu

Mississippi Valley State University is one of the leading Historical Black Colleges and Universities (HBCU) in the south. This black college prepares students for life following school, training graduates with skills designed for success. MVSU faculty, counselors and staff are present to develop skills at undergraduate and graduate levels. MVSU is a leader amongst African American universities, with curriculum tailored for a successful education and career.

Morehouse College
Year Founded: 1867
Atlanta, Georgia
(404) 215-2632
www.morehouse.edu

Morehouse College is one of the Historical Black Colleges & Universities in the United States and is known for producing African-American leaders. Many Black Colleges and African American Universities are considered HBCU. However, Morehouse College is the only all-male African American HBCU. It came into distinction internationally under Dr. Benjamin E. Mays, a mentor to Dr. Martin Luther King, Jr., the leader of the civil rights movement.

Morgan State University
Year Founded: 1867
Baltimore, MD
(410) 319-3333
www.morgan.edu

Morgan State University is the largest of the Historical Black Colleges and Universities (HBCU) in Maryland and a designated public urban university. A historically black college, Morgan State has a diverse student body of all socio-economic backgrounds. While a public African American university, Morgan State is not part of the University System of Maryland. Morgan State offers several graduate programs, including an African American studies degree.

Morris Brown College
Year Founded: 1881
Atlanta, Georgia
(404) 220-0270
www.morrisbrown.edu

Founded in 1881 and considered a historically black college, Morris Brown College is one of 105 Historical Black Colleges and Universities (HBCU) in the United States. Located near Atlanta, this African American university offers technology programs, scientific research opportunities and a liberal arts education to African American men and women in a small classroom setting. Among notable alumni are business leaders and former and current NFL athletes.

Morris College
Year Founded: 1908
Sumter, S.C.
803-775-9371
www.morris.edu

Known as South Carolina's Best Kept Secret, Morris College helps students using traditional Christian values. This four-year private school is part of HBCU and former WWII Tuskegee Airman Dr. Leroy Bowman is an alum. Like other black colleges and African American universities, Morris College uses a Baptist foundation to promote leadership and community activism. Historical black colleges & universities like Morris provide college educations to underprivileged via financial aid programs.

Norfolk State University
Year Founded: 1935
Norfolk, Virginia
804-683-8600
www.nsu.edu

For 75 years, Norfolk State University has served as a HBCU and member of the Thurgood Marshall Scholarship Fund. Boasting one of the largest student bodies among black colleges and African American universities in Virginia, Norfolk State offers two doctorates, 15 masters and 36 undergraduate degrees. Norfolk State University strives to offer the highest quality yet most affordable education throughout all historical black colleges & universities.

North Carolina A&T State University
Year Founded: 1891
Greensboro, North Carolina
919-334-7500
www.ncat.edu

North Carolina A&T State University is the largest public HBCU (Historical Black Colleges & Universities) in North Carolina. Boasting one of the largest enrollments among black colleges and African American universities, NC A&T offers nationally-ranked degree programs in engineering and a major partnership with NASA. North Carolina A&T State University is one of the most sought after of all black colleges.

North Carolina Central University
Year Founded: 1910
Durham, North Carolina
919-560-6100
www.nccu.edu

Boasting the #1 public HBCU ranking by US News & World Report two years in a row, North Carolina Central University is a prominent member of Historical Black Colleges & Universities. Offering over 80 undergraduate and 40 graduate degrees, North Carolina Central University provides students one of the biggest varieties of educational opportunities among black colleges and African American universities in North Carolina.

Oakwood University
Year Founded: 1896
Huntsville, Alabama
(205) 726-7000
http://www.oakwood.edu

Oakwood University, a private HBCU, is ranked among the best Historical Black Colleges & Universities. Among black colleges, Oakwood is a leader in preparing students for medical professions. Extra-curricular activities include an award-winning choir and championship sports teams. The alumni of Oakwood, including musicians Little Richard and Brian McKnight, civil rights activists, politicians and a number of evangelists, help distinguish it as one of the nation's top African American universities.

Paine College
Year Founded: 1882
Augusta, GA
(706) 821-8200
www.paine.edu

Founded by the United Methodist Church, Paine College is a small HBCU located in Augusta, Georgia. Providing quality liberal arts education is its mission, and like many black colleges and African American universities, Paine instills ethical and spiritual values into graduates. Among the oldest historical black colleges & universities, Paine boasts a long list of notable alumni, including Shirley McBay, the first African-American Dean at MIT, and author, film writer Frank Yerby.

Paul Quinn College
Year Founded: 1872
Dallas, Texas
214-376-1000
www.pqc.edu

With the distinction of being the oldest among Historical Black Colleges & Universities in Texas, Paul Quinn College is a private, HBCU located in Dallas. Started by the African Methodist Episcopal church, Paul Quinn College has educated students based on core Christian principles for over 138 years. Paul Quinn College strives to provide a quality, affordable liberal arts education common among black colleges and African American universities.

Philander Smith College
Year Founded: 1877
Little Rock, Arkansas
501-375-9845
www.philander.edu

Like many black colleges and African American universities across the country, Philander Smith College was founded on the principles of educating recently freed slaves. As a four-year undergraduate HBCU, Philander Smith College offers major and minor degree programs in business, education, social sciences, arts and physical sciences. Philander Smith College is known among Historical Black Colleges & Universities as having the youngest HBCU president, Dr. Walter M. Kimbrough.

Prairie View A&M University
Year Founded: 1876
Prairie View, Texas
409-857-3311
www.pvamu.edu

Prairie View A&M University has been educating students in the deeply rooted traditions of an exemplary HBCU. Striving to be best among Historical Black Colleges & Universities in Texas, Prairie View offers a variety of degrees. Prairie View A&M University is known among Texas black colleges and African American universities as one of three institutions designated as first-class by the Texas constitution.

Rust College
Year Founded: 1866
Holly Springs, Mississippi
601-252-4661
www.rustcollege.edu

One of ten Historical Black Colleges & Universities founded before 1868 and still operating, Rust College continues to educate students in the values of the United Methodist Church and HBCU. Using a fast-paced 8-week semester system not typically found among black colleges and African American universities, Rust College offers associates and bachelor degrees in 16 areas of study, including Biology, Business and Computer Science.

Saint Paul's College
Year Founded: 1888
Lawrenceville, VA
804-848-3111
www.saintpauls.edu

Saint Paul's College is a four-year HBCU situated on 185 acres in Lawrenceville, Virginia. Although smaller than most Black Colleges and African American Universities, Saint Paul's College focuses on leadership skills development in their students. With degrees in liberal arts, business and mathematics, Saint Paul's College is the only college among Historical Black Colleges and Universities to offer a residential Single Parent Support System.

Savannah State University
Year Founded: 1890
Savannah, Georgia
(912)358-4778
www.savannahstate.edu

Savannah State University is known as the oldest of the Historical Black Colleges & Universities (HBCU) in Georgia. The campus is over 173 acres to hold its growing alumni enrollment. One of the very few black colleges that offer four different research centers, of the African American universities in existence, this may be the fastest growing.

Selma University
Year Founded: 1878
Selma, Alabama
(205) 872-2533
www.selmauniversity.org

Selma University, a four-year HBCU, was founded by the Baptist Theological School in 1878 and has offered religion education as its primary focus ever since. Like many black colleges and African American universities, Selma University seeks to create spiritual leaders in the African American community. Selma University has the unique distinction of being one of the few Historical Black Colleges & Universities to offer degrees in religion and bible theology.

Shaw University
Year Founded: 1865
Raleigh, NC
919-546-8200
www.shawuniversity.edu

As the oldest HBCU in the South, Shaw University has humble beginnings among Black Colleges and African American Universities. The first college organized for African Americans, Shaw University was created at the end of the Civil War to teach freedom to a new generation of students. Undergraduate and graduate degrees are offered in Education, Theology and Liberal Arts at one of the original Historical Black Colleges and Universities.

South Carolina State University
Year Founded: 1896
Orangeburg, South Carolina
800-290-5956
www.scsu.edu

South Carolina State University is a public, four-year college. Although this school is one of many Historical Black Colleges & Universities, it welcomes people of all races and ethnicities. It strives to deliver the highest standard of education possible, as do all African American universities. Graduates of this school have become scholars, just as others have from other black colleges.

Southern University at A&M College
Baton Rouge, LA
(225) 771-4500
http://web.subr.edu

Southern University at A&M College is one of the Historical Black Colleges and Universities (HBCU) that originally had less than 500 students studying in a small building. This is one of the African American Universities offering students the chance to study in the Law program. It was one of the first Black Colleges to be visited by Eleanor Roosevelt.

Southern University at New Orleans
Year Founded: 1956
New Orleans, Louisiana
504-286-5000
http://www.suno.edu/

Southern University at New Orleans is one of the Historical Black Colleges and Universities (HBCU) offering comprehensive curriculums tailored to the cultural and educational needs of the New Orleans metro area. Like other African American Universities, it has an Honors Program producing distinguished alumni. Though this Black College was decimated by Hurricane Katrina in 2005, has been rebuilt and renovated with new resources and refurbished facilities.

Southern University at Shreveport
Year Founded: 1967
Shreveport, Louisiana
(318) 670-6000
www.susla.edu

Southern University at Shreveport (SUSLA) is one of the Historical Black Colleges & Universities (HBCU) of the Southern University System (SUS). SUSLA, as one of the African American universities, is the third best two-year university, and has a high graduation rate. Like many black colleges, SUS has famous alumni, such as Hubert Humphrey and Shaquille O'Neal.

Spelman College
Year Founded: 1881
Atlanta, GA
(404)681-3643
www.spelman.edu

Spelman College is an all-women's liberal arts college named after Laura Spelman, wife of John D. Rockefeller. Spelman students come from all over the U.S. to attend the school, which is part of the Historical Black Colleges & Universities (HBCU). Famous alumni of this black college include Bernice Johnson Reagon and actress LaTanya Richardson. African American universities like Spelman help black women attain quality educations.

St. Augustine's College
Year Founded: 1867
Raleigh, North Carolina
(919) 516-4200
www.st-aug.edu

St. Augustine's College is one of the Historical Black Colleges and Universities (HBCUs) founded in 1867 by Episcopal clergy for the education of freed slaves. This private institution serves the African American students of North Carolina and the United States. The college offers a degree in film production and it was the first HBCU operating its own commercial radio and television stations.

St. Philip's College
Year Founded: 1898
San Antonio, TX
(210) 531-359
http://www.alamo.edu/spc/

Founded as St. Philip's Normal and Industrial School, St. Philip's College is an African American University in the Texas Alamo Community College District that offers Liberal Arts and Applied Technology courses. Though originally opened to educate emancipated slaves, today this Black College is the only federally designated Historical Black College and University (HBCU) and Hispanic-serving institution with this diverse population.

Talladega College
Year Founded: 1867
Talladega, Alabama
(205) 362-0206
www.talladega.edu

Talladega College is distinguished to be the oldest of the African American universities in the state of Alabama. Talladega College is an accredited liberal arts institution and one of relatively few Historical Black Colleges & Universities (HBCUs) in the US. Talladega College maintains, as all black colleges do, a tradition of educating its students by offering workshops, forums and lectures by a diverse array of leaders.

Tennessee State University
Year Founded: 1912
Nashville, Tennessee
(615) 963-5000
www.tnstate.edu

Tennessee State University, while undergoing numerous changes since its founding, is one of 105 Historical Black Colleges & Universities (HBCU) in the US. Located in Nashville, TSU is a comprehensive land-grant university, offering many degrees, including numerous doctoral programs. TSU has a history of promoting athletics as exemplified by it being the first of the black colleges/African American universities to win a national basketball title.

Texas Southern University
Year Founded: 1947
Number of Students: 11,550
Houston, Texas
(713) 527-7011
www.tsu.edu

As one of the largest HBCU's, Texas Southern University had bold beginnings among black colleges and African American universities. In 1946, after being declined admission to University of Texas Law School, Meman Sweatt won a lawsuit, resulting in the creation of the first African American law school in Texas. Among Historical Black Colleges & Universities, TSU is popular and offers programs in business, education, law, science and technology.

Texas, College
Year Founded: 1894
Tyler, Texas
(903) 593-8311
www.texascollege.edu

Texas College, one of the Historically Black Colleges and Universities, is located in Tyler, TX, and is affiliated with the Christian Methodist Episcopal Church. As a HBCU, this African American university provides quality academics to a diverse array of students, and awards baccalaureate and associate degrees. Texas College is renowned for the commitment to service at this black college, as well as for personal attention for students.

Tougaloo College
Year Founded: 1869
Number of Students: 900
Tougaloo, MS
(601) 977-7000
http://www.tougaloo.edu

Tougaloo College, the second-oldest HBCU in Mississippi, is one of the top 20 best black colleges in the nation. Renowned among African American universities for its science and engineering programs, Tougaloo is among the few historical black colleges & universities to offer doctorate degrees. The college is home to the prominent Tougaloo Art Collection and the Civil Rights Library and Archives. Notable alumni include politicians, civil rights activists, lawyers and scholars.

Tuskegee University
Year Founded: 1881
Tuskegee, Alabama
(334) 727-8011
www.tuskegee.edu

A landmark African American University, Tuskegee University was founded in 1881 by Booker T. Washington and is distinguished as one of the nation's Historical Black Colleges and Universities (HBCU). Located in Tuskegee, Alabama, this private Liberal Arts institution offers a rigorous educational program to its diverse students. The faculty has included famous people like George Washington Carver, and the campus is a National Historic Landmark.

University of Arkansas at Pine Bluff
Pine Bluff, Arkansas
870-575-8000
www.uapb.edu

The University of Arkansas at Pine Bluff, the first HBCU in Arkansas, has a rich history among Black Colleges in Arkansas. Over 3,000 students, UAPB is one of the most popular African American Universities in the region. UAPB has one of the top aquaculture programs among historical black colleges & universities. The University of Arkansas at Pine Bluff offers Mathematics and Sciences degrees emphasizing computer science and industrial technology.

University of Maryland Eastern Shore
Year Founded: 1886
Princess Anne, Maryland
(410) 651-2200
www.umes.edu

The University of Maryland Eastern Shore, one of the Historical Black Colleges & Universities, is a public institution providing both graduate and undergraduate degrees. As an HBCU, the University offers quality academics to a diverse array of students, focusing on those who are first-generation college attendees. As one of the black colleges/African American universities, it provides values-based learning opportunities and a unique focus on multiculturalism.

University of the District of Columbia
Year Founded: 1851
Washington, D.C.
202-274-5000
http://www.udc.edu

Founded in 1851, the University of the District of Columbia remains the only public university in Washington, D.C. Recognized as a Historically Black College, UDC now offers 75 degree programs. In addition, this African American university also includes a community college to improve the lives of the residents of D.C. On the list of Historical Black Colleges and Universities (HBCU), UDC upholds an open admissions policy.

Virginia State University
Year Founded: 1882
Petersburg, Virginia
(804) 524-5000
www.vsu.edu

Virginia State University (VSU) was established as an African American university and is among the Historical Black Colleges and Universities (HBCUs). VSU founder, John Mercer Langston, was the first black man elected to the United States Congress. Following this example, VSU alumni are known as business leaders, artists, public servants and military officers. This black college offers a comprehensive educational program, concentrating on liberal arts, engineering, business and agriculture.

Virginia Union University
Year Founded: 1865
Richmond, Virginia
(804) 257-5600
www.vuu.edu

Established in 1865, Virginia Union University was formed to provide emancipated slaves with an opportunity for educational advancement. Four institutions merged in order to create VUU, now considered one of the nation's Historical Black Colleges & Universities (HBCU). Now culturally diverse, as are most black colleges and African American universities, VUU seeks to provide an intellectually challenging and spiritually enriching environment for its students.

Virginia University of Lynchburg
Year Founded: 1886
Lynchburg, Virginia
(434) 528-5276
www.vul.edu

Founded in 1886, Virginia University of Lynchburg is distinguished as one of the nation's 105 Historical Black Colleges & Universities (HBCU). African-American Baptists founded the coeducational black college, which is committed to relying upon Judeo-Christian values and a philosophy of self-help. The Just as all of the other black colleges and African American universities, VUL offers degrees in various fields and concentrations.

Voorhees College
Year Founded: 1897
Denmark, South Carolina
(803) 793-3351
www.voorhees.edu

Voorhees College has grown to become a private liberal arts college with a diverse student body. Voorhees College has a strong African-American heritage and is considered one of the nation's Historical Black Colleges & Universities (HBCU). Originally created as an industrial trade school for black students, just as many other black colleges and African American universities were, Voorhees now operates as a black liberal arts college.

West Virginia State University
Year Founded: 1891
Institute, West Virginia
(304) 766-3000
www.wvstateu.edu

Founded in 1891 as a land grant Black College, West Virginia State University has evolved from offering an applied education in agriculture and mechanical arts to a career-oriented curriculum. As one of the African American Universities, West Virginia State University is one of 105 Historical Black Colleges and Universities (HBCUs) in the United States that offers a range of Associate and Bachelor degrees.

Wilberforce University
Year Founded: 1856
Wilberforce, Ohio
(513) 376-2911
www.wilberforce.edu

Wilberforce University is distinguished as one of the nation's Historical Black Colleges & Universities (HBCUs). Wilberforce was the first of the African universities and participates in the United Negro College Fund as part of the black colleges. Wilberforce University now requires its students to participate in a cooperative education, where students must work as interns in order to gain practical experience to supplement their academic experience.

Wiley College
Year Founded: 1873
Marshall, Texas
(903) 927-3300
http://www.wileyc.edu

Wiley College is a historically black college in Marshall, Texas. There are many Historical Black Colleges & Universities in the United States. Wiley College, however, is one of the oldest black colleges west of the Mississippi. Like many African American universities, Wiley College played an instrumental role in the U.S. Civil Rights movement. As an HBCU today, it has a powerful debate team and instills a strong work ethic in students.

Winston-Salem State University
Year Founded: 1892
Winston-Salem, NC
(919) 750-2049
www.wssu.edu

Winston-Salem State University is among the top public comprehensive baccalaureate, black colleges of the south. Historical Black Colleges & Universities (HBCU) like Winston-Salem State are dedicated to diversity. The university is dedicated to presenting engaging curriculum through flexible modes of delivery. World renowned artist Selma Burke, who sculpted the bust of Franklin D. Roosevelt that appears on the dime, is among the esteemed graduates of Winston-Salem State University.

Xavier University at Louisiana
Year Founded: 1925
New Orleans, LA
(504) 486-7411
www.xula.edu

Xavier University at Louisiana is the only Catholic traditionally black college In America and is often referred to as the Emerald City. Xavier, one of many black colleges, is devoted to creating a just and compassionate society by preparing its students to become leaders. Historical Black Colleges & Universities (HBCU) welcome all nationalities and Xavier prides itself on its commitment to diversity.

Chapter 11

State Scholarships

THE STATE DIRECTORY provides information on grants, scholarships, and other financial aid for college students from the state, including federally-supported state programs. Please visit the sites for both your state of residence and for the states of the colleges to which you are applying.

Alabama
Alabama Commission on Higher Education
P.O. Box 302000
Montgomery, AL 36130-2000
Phone: (334) 242-1998
Toll-Free: (800) 960-7773
Toll-Free Restrictions: AL Residents Only
Fax: (334) 242-0268
Email: deborah.nettles@ache.alabama.gov or tim.vick@ache.alabama.gov
Website: http://www.ache.alabama.gov

Alaska
Alaska Commission on Postsecondary Education
P.O. Box 110505
Juneau, AK 99811-0505
Phone: (907) 465-2962
Toll-Free: (800) 441-2962
Fax: (907) 465-5316
TTY: (907) 465-3143
Email: customer_service@acpe.state.ak.us
Website: http://alaskadvantage.state.ak.us/

Arizona
Arizona Commission for Postsecondary Education
Suite 650
2020 North Central Avenue

Phoenix, AZ 85004-4503
Phone: (602) 258-2435
Fax: (602) 258-2483
Email: jsloan@azhighered.gov or acpe@azhighered.gov
Website: http://www.azhighered.gov/home.aspx

Arkansas
Arkansas Department of Higher Education
114 East Capitol
Little Rock, AR 72201-3818
Phone: (501) 371-2000
Fax: (501) 371-2001
Email: rickj@adhe.edu
Website: http://www.adhe.edu

California
California Student Aid Commission
P.O. Box 419027
Rancho Cordova, CA 95741-9027
Phone: (916) 526-7590
Toll-Free: (888) 224-7268
Fax: (916) 526-8004
Email: studentsupport@csac.ca.gov
Website: http://www.csac.ca.gov/

Colorado
Colorado Department of Higher Education
Suite 1600
1560 Broadway
Denver, CO 80202
Phone: (303) 866-2723
Fax: (303) 866-4266
Email: executivedirector@dhe.state.co.us
Website: http://highered.colorado.gov/

Connecticut
Connecticut Department of Higher Education
61 Woodland Street
Hartford, CT 06105-2326
Phone: (860) 947-1800
Toll-Free: (800) 842-0229
Fax: (860) 947-1310

STATE SCHOLARSHIPS

Email: lnegro@ctdhe.org or meotti@ctdhe.org
Website: http://www.ctdhe.org/

Delaware
Delaware Higher Education Commission
Fifth Floor
Carvel State Office Building
820 North French Street
Wilmington, DE 19801
Phone: (302) 577-5240
Toll-Free: (800) 292-7935
Fax: (302) 577-6765
Email: dhec@doe.k12.de.us or mlaffey@doe.k12.de.us
Website: http://www.doe.k12.de.us/dhec/

District of Columbia
Office of the State Superintendent of Education (District of Columbia)
State Board of Education
441 Fourth Street, NW
Suite 350 North
Washington, DC 20001
Phone: (202) 727-6436
Toll-Free: (877) 485-6751
Fax: (202) 727-2834
TTY: (202) 727-1675
Email: osse@dc.gov or sboe@dc.gov
Website: http://osse.dc.gov

Florida
Office of Student Financial Assistance (Florida)
State Department of Education
Suite 70
1940 North Monroe Street
Tallahassee, FL 32303-4759
Phone: (850) 410-5180
Toll-Free: (888) 827-2004
Toll-Free Restrictions: FL residents only
Fax: (850) 487-1809
Email: Theresa.Antworth@fldoe.org or osfa@fldoe.org
Website: http://www.floridastudentfinancialaid.org/osfahomepg.htm

Georgia

Georgia Student Finance Commission
Loan Services
2082 East Exchange Place
Tucker, GA 30084
Phone: (770) 724-9000
Toll-Free: (800) 505-4732
Fax: (770) 724-9089
Email: gsfcinfo@gsfc.org or monetr@gsfc.org
Website: http://www.gsfc.org/

Hawaii
State Postsecondary Education Commission (Hawaii)
Office of the Board of Regents
Room 209
2444 Dole Street
Honolulu, HI 96822-2302
Phone: (808) 956-8213
Fax: (808) 956-5158
Email: bor@hawaii.edu or ppang@hawaii.edu
Website: http://www.hawaii.edu/offices/bor/

Idaho
Idaho State Board of Education
P.O. Box 83720
650 West State Street
Boise, ID 83720-0037
Phone: (208) 334-2270
Fax: (208) 334-2632
Email: board@osbe.idaho.gov or tracie.bent@osbe.idaho.gov
Website: http://www.boardofed.idaho.gov/

Illinois
Illinois Student Assistance Commission
1755 Lake Cook Road
Deerfield, IL 60015-5209
Phone: (847) 948-8500
Toll-Free: (800) 899-4722
Fax: (847) 831-8549
TTY: (847) 831-8326
Email: collegezone@isac.org or jeckley@isac.org
Website: http://www.collegezone.com/

Indiana

STATE SCHOLARSHIPS

Indiana Commission for Higher Education
Suite 550
101 West Ohio Street
Indianapolis, IN 46204-1984
Phone: (317) 464-4400
Fax: (317) 464-4410
Email: jennifers@che.in.gov or kens@che.in.gov
Website: http://www.che.in.gov/

State Student Assistance Commission of Indiana
Suite 500
150 West Market Street
Indianapolis, IN 46204-2811
Phone: (317) 232-2350
Toll-Free: (888) 528-4719
Toll-Free Restrictions: IN residents only
Fax: (317) 232-3260
Email: grants@ssaci.state.in.us
Website: http://www.ssaci.in.gov/

Iowa
Iowa College Student Aid Commission
Fourth Floor
200 10th Street
Des Moines, IA 50309
Phone: (515) 725-3400
Toll-Free: (800) 383-4222
Toll-Free Restrictions: IA residents only
Fax: (515) 725-3401
Email: info@iowacollegeaid.org or keith.greiner@iowa.gov
Website: http://www.iowacollegeaid.gov/

Kansas
Kansas Board of Regents
Curtis State Office Building
Suite 520
1000 SW Jackson Street
Topeka, KS 66612-1368
Phone: (785) 296-3421
Fax: (785) 296-0983
Email: cbollig@ksbor.org or rrobinson@ksbor.org
Website: http://www.kansasregents.org/

Kentucky
Kentucky Higher Education Assistance Authority
P.O. Box 798
Frankfort, KY 40602-0798
Phone: (502) 696-7200
Toll-Free: (800) 928-8926
Fax: (502) 696-7496
TTY: (800) 855-2880
Email: inquiries@kheaa.com
Website: http://www.kheaa.com/

Louisiana
Louisiana Office of Student Financial Assistance
P.O. Box 91202
Baton Rouge, LA 70821-9202
Phone: (225) 922-1012
Toll-Free: (800) 259-5626 x1012
Fax: (225) 922-0790
Email: custserv@osfa.la.gov
Website: http://www.osfa.la.gov

Maine
Finance Authority of Maine
P.O. Box 949
Augusta, ME 04332-0949
Phone: (207) 623-3263
Toll-Free: (800) 228-3734
Fax: (207) 623-0095
TTY: (207) 626-2717
Email: education@famemaine.com
Website: http://www.famemaine.com/

Maryland
Maryland Higher Education Commission
Suite 400
839 Bestgate Road
Annapolis, MD 21401-3013
Phone: (410) 260-4500
Toll-Free: (800) 974-0203
Toll-Free Restrictions: MD residents only
Fax: (410) 260-3200
TTY: (800) 735-2258
Email: jlyons@mhec.state.md.us
Website: http://www.mhec.state.md.us/

STATE SCHOLARSHIPS

Massachusetts
Massachusetts Department of Higher Education
Room 1401
One Ashburton Place
Boston, MA 02108-1696
Phone: (617) 994-6950
Fax: (617) 727-6397
Email: cmccurdy@osfa.mass.edu or eavery@bhe.mass.edu
Website: http://www.mass.edu/

TERI College Planning Center
c/o Boston Public Library
700 Boylston Street, Concourse Level
Boston, MA 02116
Phone: (617) 536-0200
Toll-Free: (877) 332-4348
Toll-Free Restrictions: MA residents only
Fax: (617) 536-4737
Email: horton@teri.org or harge@teri.org
Website: http://www.tericollegeplanning.org/

Michigan
Student Financial Services Bureau
P.O. Box 30047
430 W. Allegan, 3rd Fl.
Lansing, MI 48909-7547
Toll-Free: (800) 642-5626 x37054
Fax: 517-241-0155
Email: sfs@michigan.gov or kiefern@michigan.gov
Website: http://www.michigan.gov/studentaid

Minnesota
Minnesota Office of Higher Education
Suite 350
1450 Energy Park Drive
St. Paul, MN 55108-5227
Phone: (651) 259-3901
Toll-Free: (800) 657-3866
Fax: (651) 642-0597
TTY: (800) 627-3529
Email: karen.buehre@state.mn.us or barb.schlaefer@state.mn.us
Website: http://www.ohe.state.mn.us/

Mississippi
Mississippi Institutions of Higher Learning
3825 Ridgewood Road
Jackson, MS 39211-6453
Phone: (601) 432-6623
Toll-Free: (800) 327-2980
Toll-Free Restrictions: MS residents only
Fax: (601) 432-6972
Email: commissioner@ihl.state.ms.us or sscott@mississippi.edu
Website: http://www.ihl.state.ms.us/

Missouri
Missouri Department of Higher Education
3515 Amazonas Drive
Jefferson City, MO 65109
Phone: (573) 751-2361
Toll-Free: (800) 473-6757
Fax: (573) 751-6635
TTY: (800) 735-2966
Email: info@dhe.mo.gov
Website: http://www.dhe.mo.gov/

Montana
Montana University System
2500 Broadway
P.O. Box 203201
Helena, MT 59620-3201
Phone: (406) 444-6570
Fax: (406) 444-1469
Email: lybrown@montana.edu or sstearns@montana.edu
Website: http://www.mus.edu/

Nebraska
Coordinating Commission for Postsecondary Education
(Nebraska)
Suite 300
140 North Eighth Street
P.O. Box 95005
Lincoln, NE 68509-5005
Phone: (402) 471-2847
Fax: (402) 471-2886
Email: angela.dibbert@nebraska.gov or marshall.hill@nebraska.gov
Website: http://www.ccpe.state.ne.us/PublicDoc/CCPE/Default.asp

STATE SCHOLARSHIPS

New Hampshire
New Hampshire Postsecondary Education Commission
3 Barrell Court
Suite 300
Concord, NH 03301-8543
Phone: (603) 271-2555
Fax: (603) 271-2696
TTY: (800) 735-2964
Email: pedes@pec.state.nh.us
Website: http://www.state.nh.us/postsecondary/

New Jersey
Higher Education Student Assistance Authority (New Jersey)
P.O. Box 540
Four Quakerbridge Plaza
Trenton, NJ 08625-0540
Phone: (609) 588-3226
Toll-Free: (800) 792-8670
Fax: (609) 588-7389
TTY: (609) 588-2526
Email: clientservices@hesaa.org or amaglione@hesaa.org
Website: http://www.hesaa.org/

New Jersey Commission on Higher Education
20 West State Street
P.O. Box 542
Trenton, NJ 08625-0542
Phone: (609) 292-4310
Fax: (609) 292-7225
Email: valerie.giraldi@che.state.nj.us or marguerite.beardsley@che.state.nj.us
Website: http://www.state.nj.us/highereducation/index.htm

New Mexico
New Mexico Higher Education Department
1068 Cerrillos Road
Santa Fe, NM 87505-1650
Phone: (505) 476-8400
Toll-Free: (800) 279-9777
Fax: (505) 476-8453
TTY: (800) 659-8331
Email: highered@state.nm.us or carlottam.abeyta@state.nm.us
Website: http://hed.state.nm.us/

New York
New York State Higher Education Services Corporation
99 Washington Avenue
Albany, NY 12255
Phone: (518) 473-1574
Toll-Free: (888) 697-4372
Fax: (518) 474-2839
TTY: (800) 445-5234
Email: webmail@hesc.org or rkermani@hesc.org
Website: http://www.hesc.org/

North Carolina
North Carolina State Education Assistance Authority
P.O. Box 13663
Research Triangle Park, NC 27709-3663
Phone: (919) 549-8614
Toll-Free: (866) 866-2362
Toll-Free Restrictions: NC residents only
Fax: (919) 549-8481
Email: robbie@ncseaa.edu or information@ncseaa.edu
Website: http://www.cfnc.org/

North Dakota
University System (North Dakota)
State Student Financial Assistance Program
Department 215
600 East Boulevard Avenue
Bismarck, ND 58505-0230
Phone: (701) 328-4114
Fax: (701) 328-2961
Email: peggy.wipf@ndus.edu
Website: http://www.ndus.edu/

Ohio
Ohio Board of Regents
State Grants and Scholarships Department
36th Floor
30 East Broad Street
Columbus, OH 43215
Phone: (614) 752-9475
Toll-Free: (888) 833-1133
Fax: (614) 752-5903
Email: cfoust@regents.state.oh.us
Website: http://www.uso.edu

STATE SCHOLARSHIPS

Oklahoma
Oklahoma State Regents for Higher Education
Suite 200
655 Research Parkway
Oklahoma City, OK 73104
Phone: (405) 225-9100
Toll-Free: (800) 858-1840
Fax: (405) 225-9230
Email: communicationsdepartment@osrhe.edu or rrichardson@osrhe.edu
Website: http://www.okhighered.org/

Oregon
Oregon Student Assistance Commission
Suite 100
1500 Valley River Drive
Eugene, OR 97401
Phone: (541) 687-7400
Toll-Free: (800) 452-8807
Fax: (541) 687-7414
Email: public_information@mercury.osac.state.or.us
Website: http://www.osac.state.or.us/

Oregon University System
P.O. Box 3175
Eugene, OR 97403-0175
Phone: (541) 346-5700
Fax: (541) 346-5764
TTY: (541) 346-5741
Email: maggie_bice@ous.edu or melanie_bennett@ous.edu
Website: http://www.ous.edu/

Pennsylvania
Office of Postsecondary and Higher Education (Pennsylvania)
State Department of Education
12th Floor
333 Market Street
Harrisburg, PA 17126-0333
Phone: (717) 787-5041
Fax: (717) 772-3622
TTY: (717) 783-8445
Email: lspangler@state.pa.us or dtandberg@state.pa.us
Website: http://www.pdehighered.state.pa.us/higher/site/default.asp

Pennsylvania Higher Education Assistance Agency
1200 North Seventh Street
Harrisburg, PA 17102-1444
Phone: (717) 720-2800
Toll-Free: (800) 692-7392
Toll-Free Restrictions: PA residents only
Fax: (717) 720-3914
TTY: (800) 654-5988
Email: granthelp@pheaa.org or loanhelp@pheaa.org
Website: http://www.pheaa.org/

Rhode Island
Rhode Island Higher Education Assistance Authority
Suite 100
560 Jefferson Boulevard
Warwick, RI 02886-1304
Phone: (401) 736-1100
Toll-Free: (800) 922-9855
Fax: (401) 732-3541
TTY: (401) 734-9481
Email: info@riheaa.org
Website: http://www.riheaa.org/

Rhode Island Office of Higher Education
The Hazard Building
74 West Road
Cranston, RI 02920
Phone: (401) 462-9300
Fax: (401) 462-9345
TTY: (401) 462-9331
Email: ribghe@ribghe.org or amessier@ribghe.org
Website: http://www.ribghe.org/

South Carolina
South Carolina Commission on Higher Education
Suite 200
1333 Main Street
Columbia, SC 29201
Phone: (803) 737-2260
Toll-Free: (877) 349-7183
Fax: (803) 737-2297
Email: cbrown@che.sc.gov or frontdesk@che.sc.gov
Website: http://www.che.sc.gov/

STATE SCHOLARSHIPS

South Dakota
South Dakota Board of Regents
Suite 200
306 East Capitol Avenue
Pierre, SD 57501-2545
Phone: (605) 773-3455
Fax: (605) 773-5320
Email: info@sdbor.edu
Website: http://www.sdbor.edu/

South Dakota Board of Regents
Suite 200
306 East Capitol Avenue
Pierre, SD 57501-2545
Phone: (605) 773-3455
Fax: (605) 773-5320
Email: maryt@sdbor.edu or info@sdbor.edu
Website: http://www.sdbor.edu/

Tennessee
Tennessee Higher Education Commission
Parkway Towers
Suite 1900
404 James Robertson Parkway
Nashville, TN 37243-0830
Phone: (615) 741-3605
Fax: (615) 741-6230
Email: lovella.carter@tn.gov
Website: http://www.state.tn.us/thec/

Texas
Texas Higher Education Coordinating Board
P.O. Box 12788
Austin, TX 78711-2788
Phone: (512) 427-6101
Toll-Free: (800) 242-3062
Toll-Free Restrictions: Outside Austin Metro Area
Fax: (512) 427-6127
Email: grantinfo@thecb.state.tx.us
Website: http://www.thecb.state.tx.us/

Utah
Utah System of Higher Education
State Board of Regents
60 South 400 West
Salt Lake City, UT 84101-1284
Phone: (801) 321-7103
Fax: (801) 321-7156
Email: jcottrell@utahsbr.edu
Website: http://www.utahsbr.edu/

Vermont
Vermont Student Assistance Corporation
10 East Allen Street
P.O. Box 2000
Winooski, VT 05404-2601
Phone: (802) 655-9602
Toll-Free: (800) 642-3177
Fax: (802) 654-3765
TTY: (800) 281-3341
Email: info@vsac.org
Website: http://www.vsac.org/

Virginia
State Council of Higher Education for Virginia
James Monroe Building
Ninth Floor
101 North 14th Street
Richmond, VA 23219
Phone: (804) 225-2600
Fax: (804) 225-2604
Email: KirstenNelson@schev.edu or todmassa@schev.edu
Website: http://www.schev.edu/

Washington
Washington State Higher Education Coordinating Board
P.O. Box 43430
917 Lakeridge Way
Olympia, WA 98504-3430
Phone: (360) 753-7800
Fax: (360) 753-7808
Email: info@hecb.wa.gov or belmav@hecb.wa.gov
Website: http://www.hecb.wa.gov/

CPSIA information can be obtained at www.ICGtesting.com
Printed in the USA
BVOW02s0544061213

338185BV00001B/1/P